INDIA *For* ENTREPRENEURS

A Practical Launch Guide

CA PRANAV DAMANIA

ABOUT THE AUTHOR

Chartered Accountant (CA) since 1997
Company Secretary (CS) since 2001
Registered Insolvency Professional
ACCA UK – DIP (IFR) Certified
Founder – Consult Insolvency
Promoter – WIN Corporate Advisors

Mr. Pranav Damania has been a qualified Chartered Accountant since 1997 and became a Company Secretary in 2001. He has served in the industry for more than four years at the start of his career, which includes working with reputed business groups, and thereafter, he started the practice which focuses on Taxation, Cross-border Transactions, Virtual CFOs, Transaction services, auditing and assurance, and valuation, amongst the few. He has cleared ACC UK's DIP (IFR) exam and has experience dealing with globally accepted accounting standards to understand the prevalent reporting system globally. He has more than 25 years of practice as a Chartered Accountant. He is also a certified valuer from ICAI. He is also a Registered Insolvency Professional helping numerous solvent companies to exit their businesses in an orderly manner and recover their invested capital. Apart from partnering with TMG and Associates, a Chartered Accountant, he acts as an advisor for Win Corporate Advisors Private Limited, which deals with all compliance requirements during all phases of the business, from incorporation to exit.

In his more than 25 years of professional journey, he has helped various businesses, from start-ups to multinational companies, to remain compliant with the regulatory environment by aligning the business with the applicable law. As the business grows, the requirements of a business also change; the challenges at the start-up and growth stages are different and need to be evaluated differently. Pranav understands these requirements and has helped the promoters of the business to solve complex financial and operational issues that an organization faces. His approach to finding and solving these complex issues has saved a lot of time and energy, brought efficiencyto the process, and conserved the organization's resources. He also advises start-ups to prepare themselves from a small setup to the journey of exit through strategic buyouts or IPOs. He has also dealt with the pre- and post-acquisition of business from buyers and sellers, which includes financial and secretarial due diligence, records inspection, and business operation.

Having dealt with various start-ups, working closely with promoters of the business, and working with the Government authority and judicial authority, he has developed a knack for

for understanding what it takes to be a successful business owner in India. Barring business exigencies or sudden external influence of factors beyond the control of promoters, he almost assures promoters of success if he follows the basic rules of the land and the success mantra of business. Apart from staying compliant, he helps the promoter to scale its business by taking care of the entire finance function of the business and designing the business reporting with the business owner, which will give an insight into the progress of the business and the corrective steps that a business owner needs to take to protect the assets of the business, and grow the business.

By providing virtual CFO services, he could understand the mindset of a hard-pressed CEO who has a jigsaw puzzle to handle and address the pain points that the CEO experiences while managing the entire company.

He advises on various issues relating to structuring and business efficiency for foreign companies that wish to enter India and be part of fastest growing economy of the world. He has significant experience dealing with foreign companies and managing the entire finance operations of Indian subsidiaries, including reporting and compliance. He has rich experience in handling auditing and assurance services, including internal and management audits. As a certified valuer, he has worked extensively on transactions between investor and investee companies. He and his team have handled various financial due diligence on behalf of funds and investors as part of the transaction services.

He is one of the early Registered Insolvency Professionals with the Insolvency and Bankruptcy Board of India. He has represented various cases before the Hon'ble National Company Law Tribunal, which deals with cases under the Insolvency and Bankruptcy Code, 2016(IBC).

Board of India. He has represented various cases before the Hon'ble National Company Law Tribunal, which deals with cases under the Insolvency and Bankruptcy Code, 2016(IBC). He has handled voluntary liquidation cases under the Companies Act and is now handling voluntary liquidation and corporate insolvency resolution processes and advisory projects under the IBC. He has achieved a milestone in respect of getting the first order of dissolution in India in 2017, in the first hearing passed by the Hon'ble NCLT Mumbai Bench for the Voluntary liquidation of the Company under Section 59 of the Insolvency and Bankruptcy Code, 2016. The entire liquidation was completed in less than 150 days.

ABOUT THE BOOK

'India Business—A Beginner's Guide' is written as a practical and accessible resource for aspiring entrepreneurs across the globe who are keen to explore business opportunities in India. Whether you're an Indian citizen or a foreign national, residing in India or abroad, this book is designed to help you navigate the Indian business ecosystem with clarity and confidence.

India is a land of entrepreneurs — from roadside tea vendors to global industrialists, the entrepreneurial spirit thrives at every level. This book acknowledges that success in India requires not just vision but also a sound understanding of the legal and regulatory environment.

With India's unique value proposition of scale, cost-efficiency, and a vibrant consumer base, it offers immense potential for those willing to take the leap. However, launching and operating a business in India also comes with a complex set of rules and compliance requirements.

This guide aims to simplify those complexities. It walks you through essential decisions—from choosing the right business entity to understanding licenses, HR and labor laws, compliance obligations, and financing options.

Whether you're entering the service sector, tech development, or outsourcing, this book ensures you're equipped with the foundational knowledge to succeed.

The guidance provided here draws from years of hands-on experience with both Indian and foreign businesses. It is gender-neutral, industry-agnostic, and tailored to the real-world challenges and opportunities of the Indian business landscape.

I hope this book becomes your trusted companion as you embark on your entrepreneurial journey in one of the world's most dynamic economies.

Who this book is for

This book is for all those who want to be entrepreneurs and start a business by choice to create value in society. Those who have a brilliant idea but don't know how and where to start to implement those ideas. This book is an attempt to give them the flying start they need to chase their dream of success in business.

By following the basics of a successful business, an entrepreneur can easily solve business challenges by sticking to the Principles laid down in this book.

This book will guide a person, whether in India or any part of the world, who wants to set up a business in India. It gives an idea of the laws that are applicable in India and information about the regulators who administer such laws. The parliamentary and judiciary setup will also give an idea of how the country is managed and the justice system prevalent in India. It also covers all three phases of the business: the setup, growth, and exit phases.

This book will kickstart the journey of entrepreneurship in India with a right set up. One who start well, sticks to the basics of business, observes financial discipline and stays compliant with the applicable laws will surely write his name as a successful businessowner in the history of India.

While an expert guide can be obtained for any specific industry or the laws surrounding those industries, the basic tenets enumerated in this book ensure that the basics are fundamentally clear and can give a clear vision of becoming a successful entrepreneur.

This book is for entrepreneurs who are willing to learn from others' wisdom and act accordingly. Just getting knowledge is half the job done, but having implemented that knowledge is a job fully done. This book will give enough confidence to the entrepreneur sitting on the sidelines to take the courage to start a business in India, as all his basic questions are answered here.

All the best to the ever-growing entrepreneurs who have a passion for creating huge value in society.

Foreword

“This book reminds me of my own journey as an entrepreneur.”

When I started my business, I made my share of mistakes—and learned valuable lessons from each one. This book is a valuable asset for any entrepreneur who is ready to take the leap but may feel overwhelmed by the complexities of starting a business in India.

What makes this book stand out is how clearly it highlights the often-overlooked yet essential compliance requirements. As entrepreneurs, we tend to focus solely on business growth, unintentionally ignoring the legal and regulatory aspects that are just as crucial for long-term success.

Pranav has done an excellent job of demystifying these compliance requirements in a simple, easy-to-understand manner. I highly recommend this book to every aspiring entrepreneur looking to build a strong, compliant foundation for their business journey.

Umang Naik
Founder – Cloudlabs Inc
USA, India, Canada.

“I’ve had the pleasure of knowing Pranav Damania for over a decade now — and in all that time, one thing has remained constant: his unwavering commitment to excellence. Whether it's his integrity, depth of knowledge, or sharp understanding of the business landscape, Pranav consistently sets the benchmark.

As a seasoned Chartered Accountant and Company Secretary, he brings not just credentials, but years of hands-on experience working with everyone from lean start-ups to large, complex multinationals. This book is a natural extension of that journey — a culmination of the insights he’s gathered while helping countless businesses find their footing in India’s ever-evolving ecosystem.

What truly sets this book apart is its clarity, simplicity, and real-world relevance. It doesn't read like a dry regulatory manual. Instead, it feels like you’re being guided by someone who genuinely wants you to succeed — someone who’s walked the path and is now lighting the way for others.

Whether you're just starting out or scaling something bigger, this book will be your go-to reference and a trusted companion. Pranav’s deep care for empowering entrepreneurs comes through on every page. It’s more than a guide — it’s a strategic partner for anyone serious about building “a business that’s not only successful, but also compliant and resilient.

“I genuinely believe this book will inspire and support the next generation of business leaders in India — just like Pranav has inspired so many of us along the way.

Lalit Chatnani
Director - Sony Picture Films India and
Crunchyroll India.

"This book is an essential read for anyone aspiring to become an entrepreneur and build a business in India that creates lasting value. It offers a practical and empowering roadmap for anyone with a powerful idea but unsure of how to begin, especially within the unique legal and regulatory landscape of India. With a strong focus on fundamentals, compliance, and execution, this book will give you the clarity, direction, and motivation needed to turn your vision into a successful venture."

Mitesh Damania
Entrepreneur turned startup investor.
Founder - Naturefuture.

“Refreshing read on basics of business building in India. **From Confluence (Kumbh) to Capitalism, this book takes the reader on a joyous ride of entrepreneurship.”**

Sunder Nookala
General Partner - Equirus InnovateX Fund.

I've known Pranav for a long time now, and I can say with confidence that **whenever he chooses to write, it's bound to offer real value—especially to young entrepreneurs with that relentless drive to build something from the ground up.** Pranav has lived up to that expectation. Reading this book took me back to my early days—filled with excitement, ambition, and that all-too-familiar uncertainty about how to navigate the climb toward building a successful business. This book is a thoughtful companion for anyone starting that journey.

Suhrid Sanghavi
Managing Director - Beico Group.

ACKNOWLEDGEMENTS

E = mc2, where E = Energy, is a fundamental principle of science given by the great scientist Albert Einstein. Most scientific inventions have taken place around this formula. Rightfully, Einstein has been given the Time Person of the Century award.

Even after receiving so many accolades, Einstein was always grateful for all the support he got from living and non-living things that contributed to his success. **A man is made up of the contributions of many living and non-living persons and things in his life.**

A divine person who assists individuals in realizing their true potential by activating the immense energy within themselves is known as a Guru. I bow down to all the Gurus in my life for the divine as well as the physical knowledge I gained from them.

This book is dedicated to all my mentors, seniors, and, most importantly, my clients who have successfully run their businesses based on the fundamental principles of hard work, business acumen, and adaptability in their business and personal lives.

I will always be grateful to my coach, Gaurav Arora, who believed in me and inspired me to write the book.

Lastly, I will always be indebted to the unfiltered and selfless love I received from my parents, wife, and son. They have sacrificed their time to support me in my venture.

How can I forget my motherland, India? Therefore, **this book is a tribute to my motherland, which has always believed in "Vasudhaiva Kutumbakam," which means the entire world is one family.** It embraces people from all over the world and treats them as one family.

DISCLAIMER

This book presents the factual part of India, which needs an update as India grows. It also outlines various laws generally applicable to the business entity and gives an overview of various tax and regulatory authorities that administer the applicable laws in India. Therefore, one should keep updating oneself with changes in the law. The information contained in this book is for informational purposes only and should not be construed as professional advice. Consult with a qualified professional for any specific needs or concerns.

This book is also a work of fiction. Names, characters, businesses, places, events, and incidents are either the products of the author's imagination or used fictitiously. Any resemblance to actual persons, living or otherwise, or actual events is purely coincidental.

PROLOGUE

The ancient waters of the Triveni Sangam shimmered under the golden rays of the setting sun, their currents flowing with the weight of a hundred million prayers. These waters had witnessed empires rise and fall, washing away the sins of countless devotees through the millennia. And now, as the preparations for Mahakumbh—an event that happens just once every 144 years—reached fever pitch, these sacred waters were about to witness the birth of a new empire.

Not one built of stone and mortar but one forged in the furnace of innovation, ambition, and brotherhood.

TABLE OF CONTENTS

CHAPTER

01

A LAND OF OPPORTUNITY

"In business, as in life, the greatest victories are achieved not by those who never fall, but by those who rise each time they fall."

The words echoed in Rohan's mind as his flight began its descent into Prayagraj. Through the small window, he could see the sprawling city, the majestic rivers, and the sea of humanity that had gathered for Mahakumbh. His heart raced with anticipation, not just for the spiritual cleansing the holy dip promised but also for the reunion with his brothers, Jay and Vijay.

Rohan Sharma did not believe in coincidences. The businessman in him sought patterns, connections, and opportunities where others saw random events. So when the idea of meeting his brothers during Mahakumbh first crystallized, he recognized it for what it was—destiny.

At 35, Rohan had already weathered two business failures and built two successful enterprises—a wholesale distribution network for telecom products that spanned three states and a manufacturing unit for CCTV cameras. His salt-and-pepper beard and the fine lines around his eyes spoke of battles fought and lessons learned. But it was the fire in his eyes that revealed his true character—unwavering determination.

As Rohan collected his luggage, his phone buzzed with a message from Jay: "Landed. Terminal 1. Where are you, big brother?"

Jay, the youngest of the three cousins, was a prodigy. At 23, he was completing his final year in Computer Science at Chennai Engineering College. Brilliant, idealistic, and somewhat naive about the harsh realities of business, Jay possessed the technical genius that could revolutionize industries—if properly guided.

"Terminal 2. Meet you at the central concourse in 15," Rohan replied, smiling to himself.

Thirty minutes later, as Rohan and Jay embraced, another flight touched down. Vijay Kumar, their middle cousin, stepped onto Indian soil for the first time in three years. At 28, Vijay had already made a name for himself in Silicon Valley as a consultant for startups specializing in supply chain optimization. American-educated but Indian at heart, Vijay represented the bridge between two worlds—Eastern values and Western business acumen.

"The Three Musketeers reunite!" Vijay exclaimed, dropping his bags to embrace his cousins. The terminal echoed with their laughter, drawing curious glances from passersby.

For a moment, they stood together, drinking coffee in each other's presence. Three men from the same family tree, each shaped by different environments, now stand at the confluence of their destinies, just as the three sacred rivers met at Triveni Sangam.

"This is no ordinary reunion," Rohan said, his voice dropping to a reverent whisper. **"This is Mahakumbh—an event that happens once in 144 years. The stars themselves have aligned for us to meet here, to take the holy dip together, and to forge our future."**

The gravity of his words settled over them, creating a moment of profound silence amidst the chaos of the airport.

"Speaking of forging futures," Jay said, breaking the spell, "Vijay and I have something to discuss with you. A business idea that could change everything."

Rohan smiled knowingly. "That's why I came prepared." He patted his leather briefcase. "Let's call this 'Business Bootcamp with Brother Rohan.' Three days to shape your vision into a reality."

As they exited the airport into the warm afternoon, the energy of Mahakumbh enveloped them—millions of souls unified in purpose and faith. The air vibrated with chants and prayers, with the promise of spiritual rebirth.

"Look around you," Rohan gestured broadly at the magnificent organization of the massive event. "If India can manage the largest human gathering in history—60 crore people over 45 days—imagine what three determined Indian entrepreneurs can achieve."

Their taxi driver, overhearing Rohan's words, chimed in: "Sir, you speak the truth. India is no longer the land of snake charmers. Today, we charm the world with our technology, our business minds, our innovation."

Vijay leaned forward, intrigued. "You seem to know a lot about business for a taxi driver."

The man grinned in the rearview mirror. "I have an MBA, sir. I run this taxi service as a side business. Twenty vehicles, all managed through an app I developed myself. In today's India, everyone is an entrepreneur at heart."

The three brothers exchanged glances of surprise and admiration.

"That's the India I want to tell you about," Rohan said to his cousins. "A land where opportunity flows like the sacred rivers—abundant, powerful, life-giving. But like these rivers, you must know how to navigate their currents."

As their taxi wove through the crowded streets toward their hotel, Rohan began to unfold his vision of India—not as a developing nation playing catch-up but as an economic powerhouse poised to reshape the global order.

India is the seventh-largest country by land mass, but now the most populous nation on Earth. We have the largest pool of English-speaking STEM graduates in the world. By 2027, we'll surpass Japan and Germany to become the world's third-largest economy. Goldman Sachs predicts we'll be the second-largest by 2075.

Jay whistled, impressed. "The numbers are staggering."

"Numbers tell only part of the story," Rohan continued, passion rising in his voice. "What they don't capture is the spirit, the hunger, the ambition that drives our nation forward. In the last decade, I've witnessed a transformation that defies imagination—from villages leapfrogging landlines to 5G, from cash-only transactions to becoming the global leader in digital payments."

The taxi stopped at a red light, and through the window, they could see a small street vendor accepting payment via a QR code stuck to his humble cart.

"See that?" Rohan pointed. "That's the real revolution. Technology democratized. Financial inclusion at scale. That vegetable seller probably transacts more digitally in a day than many small businesses did in a month just ten years ago"

Vijay nodded thoughtfully. "In Silicon Valley, everyone's talking about India's UPI system. It processes more transactions than American credit cards. It's a case study in financial innovation."

"And that," Rohan said, tapping his briefcase, "is just one of the reasons why your business idea should take root here, not elsewhere."

As they pulled up to their hotel—a modern structure with traditional architectural elements—Rohan placed a hand on each of his cousins' shoulders.

"Before we delve deeper into your business idea, let me share with you the essential tenets of a successful business that I've learned through my trials and tribulations. These are principles that apply universally but take on special significance in the Indian context."

As they settled in the hotel lobby, Rohan outlined the six fundamental pillars of business success:

"**First: Leadership.** The entrepreneur must lead with a clear vision, understand their product or service deeply, have an adaptable business plan, and most importantly, be passionately committed to their mission."

Jay nodded eagerly, absorbing every word.

"**Second: Human Resources.** No business thrives on the founder's efforts alone. You need the right people who share your vision, match your passion, and uphold strong work ethics."

"**Third: Marketing.** This is paramount. Even the most brilliant product will fail without effective marketing. Your strategy determines sales, and sales bring in the cash your business needs to survive. Brand building is essential for long-term value creation."

"**Fourth: Operations.** Efficiency is critical not just for survival but for scaling. Your operations should be smooth with minimal human intervention. Well-designed systems supported by the right tools minimize errors and create clear accountability."

"**Fifth: Finance.** This pillar can make or break any business, especially if you don't come from a financial background. The right financing mix can dramatically increase your return on investment, accelerating capital formation and multiplying profits."

"And Sixth: Compliance. Never underestimate the importance

of following regulations and paying taxes promptly. Compliant businesses avoid costly penalties and face government inquiries with confidence. Non-compliance might seem expedient in the short term, but the cost of rectification can be devastating."

Vijay absorbed these principles thoughtfully. "You've clearly learned these the hard way."

"I have," Rohan acknowledged with a wry smile. "My first business failed because I neglected several of these pillars. My current successes are built on a solid foundation. I want you both to leapfrog past the avoidable mistakes I made."

Rohan reached into his briefcase and pulled out three carefully prepared papers. "I've brought these for you—factual details about India's current economic landscape. They cover essential information about India, government policies and initiatives, and India's position as an emerging economic powerhouse."

He handed the documents to his cousins. "Review these later. They'll give you concrete data to support what might otherwise seem like patriotic enthusiasm on my part."

As they checked into their rooms, Rohan made one final point: "Tonight, we rest. Tomorrow, we'll witness the spiritual majesty of Mahakumbh. But remember, this trip has a dual purpose—spiritual renewal and business foundation. By the time we part ways, you'll have a comprehensive roadmap for launching your technology venture in India."

That evening, as Jay and Vijay reviewed Rohan's meticulously prepared documents in their rooms, they felt a growing conviction that their business dream wasn't just possible—it was perfectly timed to ride the wave of India's economic transformation.

SUMMARY

The basic tenets of business

- Leadership: The entrepreneur must lead with a clear vision
- Human Resource: Equally passionate about business
- Marketing – Proper marketing will bring sales, and so will the profit
- Operation – Needs to be efficiently managed
- Finance – It can make or break a good business
- Compliance – Timely compliance brings repute and avoids the heavy cost

(AI-generated image — indicative only.)

CHAPTER

02

BUSINESS AND INDUSTRY OVERVIEW

The next morning, after a light breakfast, they boarded a taxi to the Ganga Ghat area. The streets were already teeming with pilgrims, the air electric with devotional energy. As their taxi navigated the crowded thoroughfares, Rohan seized the opportunity to continue his business mentorship.

"While we journey to our spiritual destination, let's discuss India's business and industry landscape," he said, his voice cutting through the ambient noise of the bustling city. "Understanding this terrain is crucial for positioning your venture strategically."

Jay and Vijay leaned forward, eager to absorb their cousin's insights.

"India's business ecosystem is dynamic and rapidly evolving," Rohan began. "The government's focus on reforms, infrastructure development, and promoting domestic manufacturing is creating unprecedented opportunities across sectors."

"Which sectors show the most promise?" Jay asked.

Rohan's eyes lit up at the question. "Manufacturing is experiencing a renaissance through initiatives like the National Manufacturing Policy and Production Linked Incentive scheme. The goal is ambitious—**to increase manufacturing's share of GDP to 25% by 2025."**

"Is that realistic?" Vijay wondered aloud.

"The trajectory is promising," Rohan responded. "But even more relevant to your venture is the Information Technology sector. It remains a major economic driver, with strong growth potential in emerging technologies—precisely your sweet spot with data analytics."

Rohan continued, outlining the vibrant growth in services, e-commerce, infrastructure, renewable energy, healthcare, and agriculture. As their taxi inched through traffic, he painted a comprehensive picture of India's evolving economic landscape.

An annual CAGR of 8.68% is projected through 2027. Infrastructure development is accelerating, with massive investments in roads, ports, and logistics parks. Renewable energy is surging as India pursues ambitious climate goals. The National Digital Health Blueprint is revolutionizing healthcare.

A billboard advertising a major e-commerce platform caught Vijay's attention. "What about international trade? How is India positioning itself globally?"

"Excellent question," Rohan nodded approvingly. "India has established various trade agreements globally—preferential trade agreements, free trade agreements, comprehensive economic cooperation agreements, and comprehensive economic partnership agreements with numerous countries."

As their taxi crossed a bridge overlooking the river, Rohan detailed India's import and export profiles:

India's top imports include crude petroleum, gold, coal, petroleum gas, and integrated circuits. We also import significant quantities of electronic goods, transport equipment, chemicals, and textile machinery."

"And exports?" Jay prompted.

"Our export portfolio is diverse and evolving. Machinery and mechanical appliances form a major category, with small and medium enterprises driving much of this growth. The chemical industry contributes significantly to our export-import trade. Refined petroleum and oil-based products support our economy as major exports."

Rohan continued without missing a beat. "Pharmaceuticals are a key export, with many Indian firms specializing in global markets. Our automotive sector exports vehicles, including automobiles, trucks, and motorcycles, worldwide. The gems and jewelry industry remains a significant export contributor. We also export textiles, plastics, and tea, among other goods."

As they neared the riverfront, Rohan shifted to service exports his knowledge seemingly inexhaustible.

India's service exports have been growing remarkably and are expected to surpass merchandise exports by 2030. In 2021-22, India's service exports reached $254.4 billion. The IT-BPM sector leads these exports, followed by telecommunications, computer and information services, business services, and transportation. Service exports have expanded from $152 billion in 2013-14 to $341.11 billion in 2023-24, driven by IT, financial, and business services. Projections suggest we'll reach $618 billion by 2030."

The taxi finally reached their destination. As they paid the driver, Rohan concluded his overview with a striking statistic: "India exports to over 200 countries and imports from 211. We're truly integrated into the global economy."

Stepping onto the street, they were immediately enveloped by the festival atmosphere—vendors selling offerings, pilgrims singing devotional songs, sadhus in saffron robes blessing passersby.

"All this economic discussion might seem disconnected from our spiritual purpose today," Rohan acknowledged as they walked toward the riverbank. "But I believe there's profound harmony between economic prosperity and spiritual well-being. Both require discipline, vision, and ethical foundation."

Jay and Vijay nodded thoughtfully as they approached the sacred waters, their minds balancing business ambitions with the spiritual significance of their journey.

CHAPTER

03

TYPES OF ENTITIES

That evening, after their deeply moving experience at the Ganga Ghat, where millions converged for the sacred bath, the three cousins gathered in Rohan's hotel room. They had ordered dinner through Zomato, and as they waited for the food to arrive, Vijay expressed his amazement at the efficiency of India's digital ecosystem.

"From ordering food to scheduling our transportation, everything has been seamless," he marveled. "The digital infrastructure here is remarkable—certainly robust enough to support our tech venture."

Rohan nodded, pleased by his cousin's observation. India's digital revolution has created the perfect foundation for technology businesses. Now, let's discuss something fundamental to your venture's success—choosing the right type of business entity."

He cleared a space on the coffee table and laid out a diagram he had sketched earlier.

"The entity structure you choose will depend on your business plan, ownership dynamics, liability concerns, and growth strategy," Rohan explained. "Let me walk you through the options available in India."

As the aroma of their dinner filled the room, Rohan methodically outlined the various business structures:

"First, the Sole Proprietorship. A single individual owns this, and no formal registration is required. There's no separate legal identity for the business, and all risks and rewards fall on the proprietor, including personal asset exposure if the business becomes insolvent."

Jay frowned. "That sounds risky."

"It can be," Rohan agreed. "Next is the Partnership firm—two or more individuals coming together to do business. It can be registered or unregistered, but the risk profile is similar to sole proprietorship, with partners facing unlimited liability."

Vijay interrupted. "I'm guessing these first two options wouldn't work for us?"

"Correct," Rohan confirmed. "They have two major shortcomings relevant to your situation. First, foreign nationals and NRIs aren't permitted to form proprietorships or partnerships in India. Second, business transmission to the next generation becomes problematic if the proprietor or partner dies."

Their food arrived, momentarily pausing the conversation. As they unpacked the aromatic dishes, Rohan continued.

"The Limited Liability Partnership or LLP offers more protection. These are registered entities with the Ministry of Corporate Affairs and regulated by the LLP Act. You'll need to make various filings with the MCA, including financial statements. An interesting advantage is that corporate entities can become partners in an LLP."

Vijay sampled some paneer tikka while considering this option. "How does that compare to forming a company?"

"**Companies are the most popular form for businesses looking to scale significantly and attract capital,**" Rohan explained, serving himself some dal. "You typically start as a private company, which can later convert to a public company if you plan to raise capital through an IPO and list on a stock exchange."

He continued between bites, "Companies are also regulated by MCA, requiring regular filings about financial position, capital changes, and other significant decisions. The key advantage is the separation of management and ownership—industry experts can professionally manage companies without requiring them to invest heavily in the business."

"What about this One Person Company I've heard about?" Jay asked.

"That's a relatively recent innovation—designed for proprietary businesses to enjoy limited liability protection for personal assets. It's a good middle ground for sole entrepreneurs who want corporate benefits without multiple shareholders."

As they enjoyed their meal, Rohan outlined options specifically relevant to foreign entrepreneurs:

"**For businesses with foreign involvement, several structures exist.** A Liaison Office acts as a representative office, communicating between the parent company and Indian entities. It can promote the parent company's interests and build networks but cannot generate revenue in India."

"Similar to a Liaison Office, a Branch Office is an extended arm of a foreign company, not an incorporated entity. However, BOs can engage in commercial activities as the parent company's representative."

"A Project Office is designed for specific projects without indicating long-term business interest. It operates like a branch office but for particular, time-limited work."

Rohan paused to sip some water before concluding, "The most popular option for foreign companies entering India is forming a wholly-owned subsidiary or pursuing a joint venture or Limited Liability Partnership. A wholly-owned subsidiary means the foreign company incorporates a new entity held solely by the foreign company. Most foreign businesses prefer forming a private limited company as a subsidiary—it's the simplest and quickest approach."

"**For testing the market temporarily, there's also the virtual office option**—partnering with a service provider that offers employee onboarding facilities before formally establishing an entity."

After finishing their meal, they moved to the balcony to enjoy the night view of illuminated Prayagraj. Millions of lights from the Mahakumbh encampments transformed the city.

"What structure would you recommend for our venture?" Jay asked directly.

Rohan gazed thoughtfully at the glittering landscape before answering. "Based on what you've shared about your data analytics platform, with Vijay's US presence and investment, and your growth ambitions, I'd recommend a Private Limited Company structure."

He elaborated, "It offers the limited liability protection you need, allows for foreign investment, can issue ESOPs to attract talent, and provides the governance framework that future investors will expect. With Vijay as a non-resident director and you as the resident director, you'll satisfy regulatory requirements while maintaining control."

"How complicated is the incorporation process?" Vijay inquired.

"Much simpler than it once was," Rohan assured him. **"The government has digitized the entire process. With the right company secretary or legal advisor, you can complete incorporation in one to two weeks.** Exit, if ever needed, can take one to three months, depending on various factors."

As they watched a group of devotees passing below, singing bhajans with joyful abandon, Rohan reflected on the significance of their discussion.

"Structure might seem like a technical detail, but it's the skeleton of your business—it determines how you'll grow, how you'll be taxed, how you'll attract investment, and ultimately, how you'll realize value from your enterprise. Choose wisely at the beginning, and you'll avoid painful restructuring later."

Jay and Vijay nodded, appreciating the weight of this decision. Their business dream was taking concrete shape, transitioning from abstract concepts to structured reality under Rohan's experienced guidance.

SUMMARY

Private Limited Companies (PLCs) and LLPs are regulated entities that carry a much higher reputation than traditional proprietor or partnership firms. The Business's longevity and succession are guaranteed in the case of a PLC or LLP. They also offer an opportunity to own a business without effectively managing it, which can be outsourced to an industry expert to manage the business. That is how successful industrial houses create many diverse businesses with great success, as management and ownership are separate.

For an NRI or a foreign company, forming a 100% Indian subsidiary company is the simplest form of business entity. The RBI oversees the simplified investment requirements for Indian businesses.

India Entry Strategy

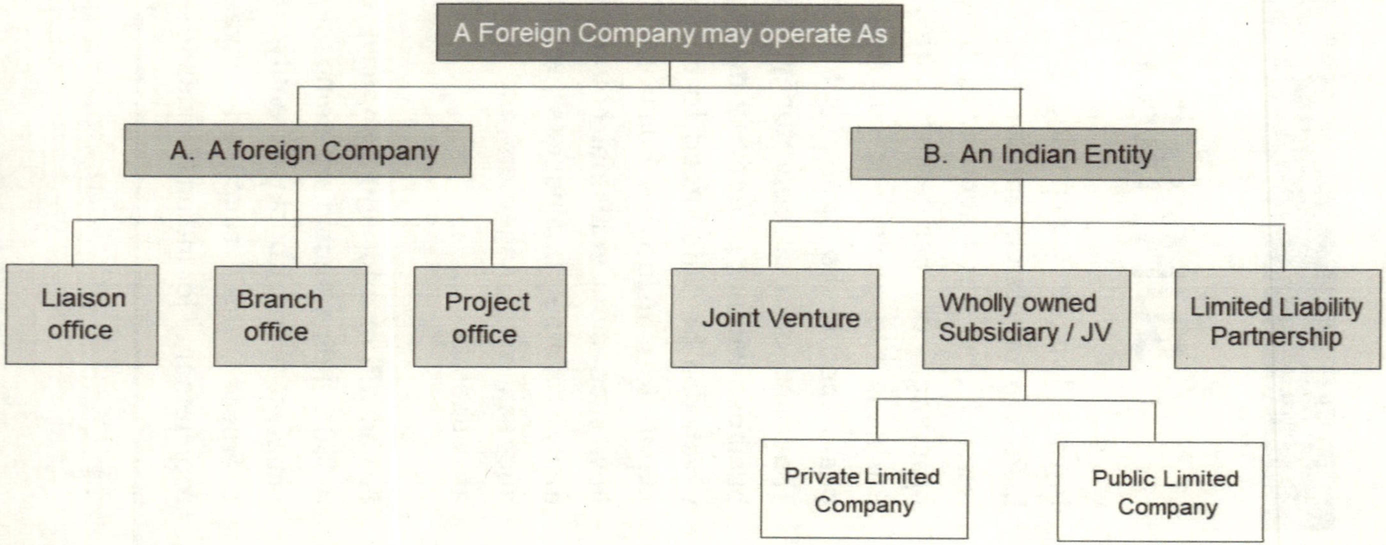

CHAPTER

04

REGULATORY FRAMEWORK

The next morning broke with the promise of another spiritually enriching day. The three cousins rose early, eager to witness the magnificent organization of Mahakumbh firsthand. After a quick breakfast, they decided to walk to the boating point rather than take a taxi—the pleasant 25-minute stroll would give them time to continue their business discussions while absorbing the vibrant atmosphere.

"Today," Rohan announced as they set out, "let's discuss something many entrepreneurs fear unnecessarily—India's regulatory framework. Understanding which regulators oversee your business activities is essential for smooth operation."

The morning air was crisp and refreshing, and the temperature was a comfortable 16 degrees. These were perfect conditions for a clear-headed discussion of complex regulatory matters.

"Regulation can seem intimidating," Rohan acknowledged, "but when you understand the underlying purpose of each regulatory body, compliance becomes strategic rather than burdensome."

As they navigated the lively streets, Rohan systematically outlined the key regulatory authorities relevant to their venture:

"First, the Ministry of Corporate Affairs—MCA is primarily concerned with administering the Companies Act, the Limited Liability Partnership Act, and the Insolvency and Bankruptcy Code. All your company registrations and filings will go through their portal. An interesting feature of the MCA system is the public inspection capability—anyone can examine documents filed by any company or LLP, which promotes transparency but also means your financial statements are publicly accessible."

They passed a group of pilgrims from South India, their distinctive attire adding to the colorful mosaic of the festival. Rohan continued once they moved past.

"Next, the Reserve Bank of India (RBI regulates foreign currency and protects India's foreign exchange. They also regulate all banks and NBFCs. Any transaction involving foreign currency, whether capital or current account, must be reported to the RBI through your Authorized Dealer Bank."

"Does that create obstacles for foreign investment?" Vijay asked, concerned about his planned investment from the US.

"Not anymore," Rohan reassured him. "**For most sectors, including information technology, prior RBI permission has**

been eliminated. You follow the prescribed reporting procedures after the investment is made. Only a few strategic sectors still require advanced approval."

A vendor selling marigold garlands called out to them, but they politely declined and continued their walk.

"The tax administration consists of two main bodies," Rohan explained. "The Central Board of Direct Taxes (CBDT) manages income tax, corporate tax, and other direct taxes. They function under the Ministry of Finance, ensuring compliance, enforcing tax laws, and developing tax policies."

"Paralleling CBDT is the Central Board of Indirect Taxes and Customs, which handles indirect taxes, including GST, customs duties, and excise duties. They also work to prevent smuggling and ensure compliance."

They paused at a crossroads, waiting for a gap in the stream of pedestrians.

Both these bodies help generate government revenue, reduce tax evasion, and enhance financial transparency. Building a good relationship with tax authorities through consistent compliance is invaluable for business stability. Income tax and corporate tax's share of revenue is higher than the indirect tax's share in total tax revenue generated by the Government."

As they continued their journey, Rohan touched on labor regulations.

Labor laws are administered primarily through the Provident Fund and Employee State Insurance organizations, which handle retirement and insurance benefits. Beyond these, you'll need to comply with regulations on gratuity, bonuses, maternity benefits, and prevention of sexual harassment in the workplace."

"Sounds complex," Jay commented.

"It can be," Rohan acknowledged, "but the government is working to consolidate various labor laws into simplified codes. And with the right HR and compliance partners, managing these requirements becomes routine."

They passed an ancient temple, its intricate carvings a reminder of India's architectural heritage. After a respectful pause, Rohan continued.

“If your business has any import or export transactions, then The Directorate General of Foreign Trade (DGFT) is the Indian government agency responsible for regulating and promoting international trade. It formulates and implements the Foreign Trade Policy, issues licenses and certifications, and provides trade-related information and assistance.”

"If your business has environmental implications, the Pollution Control Boards at the central and state levels will be relevant. They plan, implement, and monitor pollution control programs, set standards, advise governments, and conduct research."

"For businesses seeking public investment, the Securities and Exchange Board of India regulates the securities market, focusing on investor protection, fair trading practices, preventing market manipulation, and promoting market development."

"The Insolvency and Bankruptcy Board of India oversees businesses facing insolvency, regulating insolvency professionals, agencies, and information utilities. They also facilitate the liquidation of solvent companies that wish to exit and return capital to shareholders."

As they approached the river, the crowd density increased, and pilgrims converged from all directions toward the sacred waters.

"The National Company Law Tribunal resolves company disputes, handles mergers, addresses insolvency proceedings, and deals with corporate mismanagement. It's the primary adjudicating authority for corporate insolvency."

"India's judicial system operates on three levels—the Supreme Court at the apex, High Courts at the state level, and subordinate courts at the district level. Understanding this structure helps when legal disputes arise."

They reached the boating site, where thousands of devotees were already queuing for boats to take them to Triveni Sangam. Rohan managed to locate their pre-arranged private boat through the crowd.

"Finally," he said as they waited for their boat to be prepared, "intellectual property protection is crucial for technology businesses. India is a member of the World Intellectual Property Organization and protects IPRs through laws covering patents, copyrights, trademarks, industrial designs, geographical indications, plant varieties, and semiconductor integrated circuit layouts."

"What about auditing requirements?" Vijay inquired as they

boarded their small wooden boat.

"Statutory audits are mandatory for companies under the Companies Act," Rohan explained as they settled onto the wooden bench. "Tax laws require audits if turnover exceeds specified limits—currently 100 million rupees. For international businesses with associated enterprises, transfer pricing audits may be necessary to ensure arm's-length pricing in cross-border transactions."

As their boat joined the procession of vessels heading toward Sangam, Rohan concluded his regulatory overview.

"The regulatory landscape might seem overwhelming initially, but remember—you don't need to master every detail personally. You need competent professionals—a good chartered accountant, a company secretary, and eventually a compliance officer as you grow. Their expertise becomes your shield against regulatory missteps."

The boat glided through the sacred waters, carrying them toward the confluence where millions would take their holy dip. The rhythmic splash of oars created a meditative backdrop for their conversation.

"The true wisdom in regulation," Rohan reflected, watching the approaching shoreline, "is understanding that compliance isn't a burden but an investment in business longevity. **The cost of compliance is predictable and manageable.** The cost of non-compliance—penalties, reputation damage, operational disruptions—is unpredictable and potentially devastating."

As they neared Triveni Sangam, the conversation naturally shifted from business to spirituality, their minds preparing for the profound experience ahead. Yet even in this transition, there was a lesson—the successful entrepreneur must balance material pursuits with spiritual groundedness and regulatory compliance with ethical integrity.

SUMMARY

The following are major regulators and judicial authorities in India

1. Ministry of Corporate Affairs
2. Reserve Bank of India
3. CBDT and CBIC administer Direct and Indirect Tax
4. Courts and Tribunals
5. SEBI
6. Labour Welfare Department
7. Others

CHAPTER

05

BASIC REQUIREMENTS

After reaching the boating site, they secured an small boat to reach Triveni Sangam. As their vessel moved through the sacred waters, with three crew members expertly navigating the currents, Rohan utilized the 45-minute journey to outline the basic requirements for setting up a business in India.

The sun cast dancing reflections on the water as ancient monuments and a majestic fort passed by. The boatman pointed out historical landmarks, mentioning how India once controlled about 30% of world trade in ancient times. This historical context inspired all three brothers, kindling a shared determination to contribute to their motherland's economic resurgence.

"Now that you're both committed to launching your business soon," Rohan began, noting their enthusiasm, "let me outline the practical requirements for establishing your venture."

Despite the mesmerizing rhythm of the oars and the scenic beauty around them, Jay and Vijay listened intently as Rohan detailed the essentials:

"First, you'll need to finalize your ownership structure," Rohan explained. "Once you've chosen your entity type, you must determine exactly who owns what percentage of the business. Since Vijay is an NRI, his investment will be governed by Foreign Direct Investment regulations, requiring additional reporting and compliance with FDI rules. For Company you'll issue shares—either physical or dematerialized—to shareholders and file the necessary returns with the Ministry of Corporate Affairs."

A passing boat filled with chanting pilgrims momentarily drew their attention before Rohan continued.

"Next, determine your management structure. For companies and LLPs, the management can differ from ownership. Your management roles and responsibilities must be clearly defined in the entity's charter documents. Remember that the board of directors bears ultimate responsibility for the company's functioning."

"How does the resident director requirement work?" Vijay asked, recalling their earlier discussion.

"That's a critical point," Rohan nodded. Companies and LLPs must have at least one resident director/partner on their board. Since Jay will be based in India, he can fulfill this requirement. I've seen foreign companies operating in India appoint their country heads as resident directors to satisfy his condition."

Their boat navigated around a shallow area, the crew working in perfect coordination—a living example of effective team management that Rohan subtly noted.

"You'll need to maintain proper books of accounts and records in compliance with tax laws and the Companies Act," he continued. "The Companies Act requires keeping the accounting server in India. Your records should include accounting entries, vendor invoices, sales invoices, bank statements, tax documents, audit records, and statutory records. These must be preserved for eight years, though they can be maintained electronically."

"Every business entity needs a registered office in India to comply with tax laws and the Companies Act," Rohan explained as they passed the historic monument. "This serves as your official address for correspondence. Practically speaking, most communication now happens via email, but the physical address remains a requirement. Many service providers offer shared offices and coworking spaces that can serve as registered offices."

The boat rocked gently as a larger vessel passed nearby, prompting Rohan to pause briefly before continuing.

"Obtaining necessary licenses is essential. You'll need to apply for trade licenses and any industry-specific permits. Other crucial registrations include your Permanent Account Number, Tax Account Number, and Professional Tax registration. Fortunately, for companies and LLPs, the MCA facilitates obtaining these licenses, along with PF and ESIC registrations, during incorporation, eliminating the need for separate applications."

"What about GST registration?" Jay inquired.

"GST registration becomes mandatory once turnover exceeds 2 million rupees for services or 4 million for goods," Rohan replied. "However, I'd recommend voluntary registration from the start—it allows you to claim input tax credits on the GST you pay for business expenses, which improves cash flow."

As their boat approached the sacred confluence, Rohan added an important point specific to their business model.

"Since you'll potentially export services from India to the US, I advise obtaining an Import Export code (IEC) and Letter of Undertaking (LUT). This allows you to export services without levying GST since the services will be consumed abroad. LUTs can be obtained online through a straightforward process."

"Finally," Rohan said as the boat slowed near their destination, "companies must complete a 'commencement of business' procedure—essentially confirming your initial capital formation before you're permitted to begin operations."

The boat came to rest at Triveni Sangam Ghat, where thousands of devotees were already performing their sacred rituals. Before disembarking, Rohan summarized:

"With these foundational elements in place—ownership structure, management, resident director, proper records, registered office, necessary licenses, GST registration, and commencement of business completion—you'll be fully prepared to launch your venture legally and efficiently."

They stepped onto the sangam, their minds balancing the

practical business knowledge they'd gained with the spiritual significance of the moment before them. As they prepared for their holy dip at the confluence of the three sacred rivers—Ganga, Yamuna, and Saraswati—Rohan reflected that this physical convergence mirrored their confluence of skills, knowledge, and ambition, which would soon manifest as a thriving business.

SUMMARY

- The ownership structure needs to be finalized to accommodate all the owners or contributors to the business. This can easily be formed and modified later in the case of a private limited company or LLP.
- Management: Management and ownership can be separated to bring professional expertise to the business.
- One Resident director/partner is necessary in case of a Private Limited Company and LLP
- Every business entity needs to keep prescribed books of accounts under tax and regulatory laws in India
- Registered office is compulsory for carrying out the business
- A business entity needs to obtain a business and trade license to operate the business

CHAPTER

06

LIFE CYCLE OF BUSINESS

The experience at Triveni Sangam was profound beyond words. The three brothers had taken their holy dip with worship, remembering family members, friends, departed souls, and forefathers as their parents had instructed. The sacred waters where the three goddess rivers converged had left them feeling spiritually renewed. After capturing photographs and collecting bottles of holy water to bring home, they changed into dry clothes and began their journey back to the boating point.

As their boat sliced through the waters returning to the shore, Jay gazed thoughtfully at the endless flow of the rivers and asked, "Rohan bhai, just as humans go through life stages from childhood to old age, does business follow a similar life cycle?"

Rohan smiled approvingly at the philosophical connection. "An excellent observation, Jay. Yes, businesses indeed follow a life cycle with distinct phases, each requiring different approaches and strategies."

Despite their spiritual immersion just moments before, both Jay and Vijay leaned forward, eager to hear Rohan's insights on this topic.

"The business lifecycle begins with birth," Rohan explained, his voice carrying clearly over the sound of water lapping against the boat. "This phase involves incorporation and establishment. Like a newborn, the business is fragile, requiring careful nurturing and protection."

The boatman, who had been silent during their spiritual rituals, now listened with interest to Rohan's business wisdom.

"The growth phase follows," Rohan continued, "and this is the most critical period that demands the entrepreneur's fullest attention. **Here, the business either flourishes or falters**. Success requires sufficient capital to develop products or services and launch them effectively in the market. Wise entrepreneurs maintain buffer capital for marketing efforts and product improvements."

A passing boat filled with pilgrims called out blessings, momentarily interrupting Rohan's discourse. After acknowledging them with folded hands, he resumed.

"The timeline to positive cash flow varies greatly depending on industry, development cycles, working capital requirements, and contingency needs. Once the business begins generating positive cash flow, the focus shifts to scaling operations, which typically requires growth capital."

"How do we determine the right mix of financing?" Vijay asked, his financial acumen surfacing.

"That depends on your return on investment," Rohan replied. "You should carefully consider debt versus equity proportions. Since debt costs are tax-deductible, the actual cost of debt is typically lower than equity. However, too much debt creates dangerous obligations."

The boat rounded a bend, revealing the majestic skyline of Prayagraj in the distance.

"As you grow, you might need to attract private capital from Alternative Investment Funds. These AIFs—both general and sector-specific—not only provide capital but also bring expertise to accelerate growth."

"And what about going public?" Jay asked, eyes gleaming with ambition.

Rohan chuckled at his younger cousin's forward thinking. "When your company achieves substantial scale, and you're seeking liquidity options, an Initial Public Offering becomes viable. IPOs allow public participation in ownership while providing liquidity to founding shareholders through stock exchange listing."

He patted Jay on the shoulder. "And when that day comes, I'll be first in line to subscribe to your IPO. I believe in you both that much."

The boatman nodded approvingly at this expression of family support.

Vijay, ever the pragmatist, steered the conversation to less pleasant territory. "What happens if the business faces a downturn or we need to exit due to circumstances beyond our control?"

Rather than appearing discouraged by the question, Rohan seemed pleased by Vijay's foresight. "**These situations aren't abnormal**—they're part of the mature business stage, similar to human old age. As an entrepreneur, you must first assess whether the disruption is temporary. If it's worsening, several options exist to prevent value erosion."

The boat approached a shallow area, and the crew navigated carefully around it—a fitting metaphor for business navigation that Rohan didn't miss.

"First, consider merger or amalgamation with compatible companies to achieve scale and technological advantage, potentially giving your business new life."

"Second, partial or complete sale to a strategic partner might be appropriate if you believe the business has peaked and growth is flattening. The right partner might take it to levels you couldn't reach independently."

"Third, orderly liquidation or winding up can protect the remaining capital if prospects appear dim. The remaining funds can be repatriated to shareholders, including foreign investors like Vijay, who would be."

The boat was now nearing the shore, and their journey was almost complete, but Rohan had one final lifecycle stage to address.

"In extreme cases of continuous losses, where assets fall below liabilities—perhaps due to technological disruption devaluing your assets—insolvency becomes a reality. However, this is now recognized as a normal business outcome. The Insolvency and Bankruptcy Code provides a framework for business restructuring while preserving value and employment. Special distress funds seek to acquire such businesses for rehabilitation. If restructuring isn't viable, orderly liquidation allows entrepreneurs to exit without personal asset loss and start fresh with reputation intact."

As their boat docked, Rohan concluded, "Understanding these lifecycle stages helps you prepare for each transition. The wise entrepreneur anticipates these phases rather than being surprised by them."

They disembarked, thanking the boatman for both the physical journey and his silent respect for their discussion. As they walked from the boating point toward the busy street to find transportation back to their hotel, Jay commented, "It's remarkable how closely business lifecycles mirror human lives —birth, growth, maturity, and eventually, transition."

"Yes," Rohan agreed, "and like life itself, business success comes not from avoiding these stages but from navigating them with wisdom, preparation, and grace."

SUMMARY

Business also follows the lifecycle, which is

1. Incorporation and set up
2. Growth
3. Mature and Transition stage

Every stage of the business lifecycle requires a different level of energy and understanding from the business owners.

CHAPTER

07

HUMAN RESOURCE

After their profound experience at Triveni Sangam, the three cousins found themselves exhausted and wanting. They searched desperately for transportation back to their hotel, finally spotting an available e-rickshaw. Though slower than a conventional auto-rickshaw, they gratefully climbed aboard the battery-powered vehicle.

As the e-rickshaw hummed quietly through the crowded streets, Rohan observed how the driver skillfully navigated through impossible gaps in traffic, politely interacted with pedestrians, and maintained his vehicle with obvious care.

"Watching this driver reminds me of another crucial business resource we haven't discussed yet," Rohan said, his voice rising just enough to be heard over the street noise. "Human resources—the people who transform your vision into reality."

Despite their fatigue and hunger, Jay and Vijay recognized the importance of the topic. The slower pace of the e-rickshaw actually created a perfect opportunity for this discussion.

"Gone are the days when employees were treated merely as labor," Rohan began, gesturing toward the hardworking rickshaw driver. "In modern business, especially in technology ventures like yours, people are your greatest asset and must be treated as partners in your success."

The e-rickshaw slowed to allow a family to cross, giving Rohan a moment to organize his thoughts.

"Whether in technology or any other sector, retaining key employees—especially C-level executives and senior managers—is critical. **One effective retention tool is Employee Stock Ownership Plans or ESOPs.** These give employees ownership stakes, aligning their interests with the company's growth."

Vijay nodded thoughtfully. "That's standard practice in Silicon Valley startups."

"Exactly," Rohan continued as the vehicle resumed its journey. "I can share a relevant example. One of my CCTV camera clients is headquartered in Delaware but operates in India. Their Indian employees receive shares of the parent company listed on NASDAQ at concessional rates after completing certain tenure requirements. They can later sell these shares at market prices, creating substantial profit potential. This incentivizes performance since their gain directly connects to company success."

The e-rickshaw turned onto a quieter street, making conversation easier.

"For any business to thrive, human resources are vital to fulfilling the entrepreneur's vision. Look at the House of Tatas —they operate across diverse sectors, from steel to automobiles to technology to consumer goods. They're known as one of India's best employers because they provide benefits beyond mandatory requirements, creating a loyal, happy workforce."

Jay, who had been quietly absorbing this information, asked, "What about labour regulations? I've heard India has complex employment laws."

Rohan appreciated the practical question. India does have comprehensive labour protection. Key regulations include the Factories Act governing working conditions, safety measures, and welfare provisions; the Minimum Wages Act setting industry-specific wage floors; and the Payment of Wages Act ensuring timely, complete compensation."

The e-rickshaw driver navigated around a pothole, demonstrating the care and attention Rohan described as essential in employee management.

"Other important legislation includes the Employees' Provident Fund and Miscellaneous Provisions Act, establishing retirement funds; the Workmen's Compensation Act, providing for work-related injury compensation; and Employee State Insurance, offering health benefits to workers and their families."

As they approached their hotel, Rohan added, "The government is working to simplify these regulations by consolidating them into streamlined labour codes, which should ease compliance burdens while maintaining worker protections."

The e-rickshaw pulled up to their hotel, and the cousins paid the driver generously, thanking him for his excellent service—a small but meaningful recognition of quality work that illustrated Rohan's point about valuing human resources.

As they stepped into the hotel lobby, Rohan concluded, "Remember, in today's knowledge economy, particularly in your technology field, your competitive advantage lies not in what machines you own but in what minds you employ. Treat your future team members as true stakeholders, and they'll drive your success beyond what you could achieve alone."

The cousins nodded their agreement as they headed toward the restaurant. Their hunger now demanded immediate attention, but their minds were filled with insights about the human dimension of business success.

SUMMARY

Human resources are one of the very important contributors to the business. To keep the workforce happy and satisfied, various labor welfare measures are mandatory for an entity to follow. Additional voluntary welfare measures may be introduced to boost staff morale.".

CHAPTER

08

TAX FRAMEWORK

After showering and changing into fresh clothes, the three cousins made their way to a renowned restaurant just 150 meters from their hotel. The establishment was renowned for its authentic North Indian cuisine, and the enticing aromas wafting from the kitchen immediately confirmed they'd made an excellent choice.

They ordered generously—mixed vegetables, dal makhani, paneer tikka, garlic naan, and jeera rice—their appetites heightened by the day's spiritual and intellectual exertions. The food arrived promptly, and they ate with appreciative gusto, momentarily setting aside business discussions to savor the culinary excellence.

When the meal concluded, Rohan asked for the bill. When it arrived, Jay examined it curiously, noting the GST charges itemized at the bottom.

"You know," Jay said with a slight frown, "one of my engineering classmates told me that India has one of the highest tax burdens in the world. “He claimed that businesses here pay more than 50% in income tax and GST combined. Is that true?"

Rohan's expression remained calm, but his eyes reflected amusement at the misconception. "That's a common misunderstanding. Let me clarify India's tax framework—but on one condition."

"What's that?" Jay asked.

"You treat us to jalebis from the sweet shop next door," Rohan replied with a grin.

Jay laughed. "Deal!"

After settling the restaurant bill, they strolled to the nearby sweet shop, where the intoxicating aroma of fresh jalebis sizzling in ghee drew a steady stream of customers. As they waited for their order, Rohan began explaining India's tax system.

"First, let's address direct taxation—income tax for individuals and corporate tax for companies," Rohan began. "Individual tax rates are not among the highest globally, and in fact, the recent tax amendment brought zero tax on income up to 12 lakh Rupees."

The sweet shop owner deftly lifted golden, syrup-soaked jalebis from the fryer, the sweet aroma intensifying as they approached the counter.

"As for corporate taxes," Rohan continued, "India's rates are quite competitive internationally. While there are different tax schemes companies can choose, the most popular levies tax at 25.17% on business profits. This tax applies only to profits remaining after all business expenses and director remuneration. Furthermore, losses from previous years can be carried forward to offset profits in subsequent years."

Their jalebi order arrived—crisp, hot, and dripping with sweet syrup. They moved to a small standing table near the window. "Now, regarding Goods and Services Tax," Rohan said, blowing gently on a hot jalebi before taking a bite. "GST in India follows three primary rates—5%, 18%, and 28%—depending on the classification of goods. Services are generally taxed at 18%."

Jay took his first bite of jalebi, the crispy exterior giving way to a syrupy sweetness that momentarily diverted his attention from tax matters.

Seeing his cousin's enjoyment, Rohan continued. "But here's the critical concept your friend missed—value-added taxation. When your technology company charges 18% GST on your services, you don't pay the entire amount to the government. You can claim Input Tax Credit (ITC) for GST paid on your business expenses and capital assets like laptops."

Vijay, who had been quietly listening while enjoying his sweet, perked up. "So it's a pass-through tax?"

"Exactly," Rohan nodded. "Y**our actual GST liability is only on the value you add.** To utilize ITC, ensure you have valid vendor invoices and deal with GST-compliant suppliers who file timely returns, allowing your ITC claims to be verified."

As they savored the hot jalebis, Rohan moved to more complex aspects of taxation.

"Two other tax concepts relevant to your venture are Withholding Tax and Transfer Pricing. Withholding Tax, or TDS (Tax Deducted at Source), requires payers to deduct tax when making specified payments such as salaries, rent, professional fees, commission, or contract charges. The deductor withholds the prescribed percentage, pays the recipient the net amount, deposits the TDS with the government, and files returns. This creates a tax credit for the recipient, which they can claim when filing their income tax returns."

The sweetness of the jalebis provided a pleasant counterpoint to the technical tax discussion.

"As for Transfer Pricing," Rohan continued, "this international tax mechanism ensures each country collects appropriate tax on profits earned within its jurisdiction. It prevents the manipulation of prices in transactions between related entities in different tax jurisdictions to shift profits artificially to low-tax jurisdictions. Since you'll likely have transactions between your Indian entity and Vijay's US company, you'll need to follow Transfer Pricing guidelines to ensure transactions occur at arm's length prices."

As they finished their jalebis, Jay looked visibly relieved. "So we won't be paying 50% in taxes after all."

"Not even close," Rohan reassured him. "With proper planning and compliance, India's tax burden is reasonable and competitive. What's crucial is maintaining accurate records, filing timely returns, and working with qualified tax " professionals who understand your specific business model."

Jay ordered another round of jalebis, feeling the tax framework discussion deserved additional celebration. As they waited for the fresh batch, Vijay asked, "Are there any tax incentives specific to technology companies we should know about?"

"Several," Rohan confirmed. "**The government offers various benefits for startups and MSMEs, including tax holidays for certain periods,** accelerated depreciation on technology investments, and special deductions for research and development expenditures. Once your business plan is finalized, a good tax consultant can help structure operations to optimize your tax position legitimately."

The second round of jalebis arrived, even hotter and fresher than the first. As they enjoyed this additional indulgence, Rohan concluded, "Like these jalebis—which are sweet but not overwhelmingly so—India's tax framework seeks balance. It generates necessary revenue for public services while remaining competitive enough to attract and retain business investment. Understanding this framework isn't just about compliance; it's about strategic planning that turns tax management from a burden into a business advantage."

The cousins left the sweet shop with sticky fingers, satisfied appetites, and a much clearer understanding of India's tax landscape—a crucial piece of knowledge for their entrepreneurial journey.

SUMMARY

Tax plays a major role in the cost of any business. There is a direct tax mechanism where the tax impact is directly linked to the entity's income or profits. Tax exemption and deduction schemes are available to an entity or individual that can be used to minimize the tax bill. Under the Direct tax, there are also provisions relating to withholding tax and transfer price.

Indirect tax is a pass-through for an entity that is ultimately borne by the customer who consumes such goods or services. An entity can take the input tax credit on its purchase, and thus, it is liable to pay tax only on the value added by the entity for the product or service sold by the entity.

CHAPTER

09

FUNDING OF INDIAN BUSINESS

The next day, after a refreshing afternoon nap to recover from their spiritual exertions at Mahakumbh, the three cousins decided to venture out for tea. They found a charming tea stall nearby that served beverages in traditional clay cups called kulhads—a novelty for Vijay, who had grown accustomed to American coffee shop culture.

While Rohan ordered ginger-infused green tea for himself and Jay, Vijay opted for coffee. As they waited for their drinks, Vijay turned to Rohan with an earnest expression.

"Rohan bhai, you've shared invaluable insights about business structures, regulations, and taxation. But there's one critical aspect we haven't deeply explored yet—financing options for our venture, especially in the Indian context. You're clearly an expert at financial management; we'd greatly benefit from your wisdom."

Rohan nodded appreciatively at the request. The preparation of their beverages created a perfect backdrop for this important discussion—the careful measuring of ingredients, the controlled brewing process, and the final presentation—all echoing the precision needed in financial planning.

"Funding is indeed the lifeblood of any enterprise," Rohan began as their drinks were being prepared. "The simplest approach is committing your capital, which automatically brings seriousness and commitment to the venture. However, personal resources can only take you so far. For meaningful growth, external funding becomes essential."

Their drinks arrived in earthen kulhads, the traditional clay imparting a subtle earthy flavor that enhanced the beverages. Vijay examined his kulhad with curiosity before taking his first sip.

"Let me outline the primary funding options," Rohan continued. "First, debt financing—loans from banks, Non-Banking Financial Companies (NBFCs), or financial institutions. These can be secured against collateral, carrying lower interest rates, or unsecured, with higher rates reflecting increased lender risk.". The Government is also supporting **eligible business with a loan through banks for as high as INR 100 million** as the lower interest is burden by the Government.

Rohan blew gently on his hot tea before taking a careful sip. "Debt can be structured as term loans for capital expenditure with fixed repayment schedules, or as working capital facilities to bridge timing gaps between inventory purchase, sales, and collections."

"The advantage of working capital loans," he explained,

"is that interest applies only to the amount utilized. With proper cash flow management, you can minimize interest costs by using the facility strategically."

Jay, who had been quietly absorbing this information while enjoying his tea, asked, "What about equity funding? That seems to be the preferred route for tech startups."

"Equity capital involves selling ownership stakes," Rohan replied. "It carries the highest risk for investors but offers safety for entrepreneurs since it doesn't require fixed interest payments or return of principal. The tradeoff, of course, is dilution of ownership and control."

The hot tea had cooled enough for comfortable drinking, and they all enjoyed their beverages as Rohan continued.

India now has a vibrant private investment ecosystem. Alternative Investment Funds—family offices, angel investors, and venture capital firms—actively seek promising ventures, particularly in technology. Some funds specialize in specific sectors or stages, making them ideal partners for businesses matching their investment thesis."

Vijay found the coffee in a kulhad surprisingly delightful—the clay adding complexity to the flavor profile. "The key difference between debt and equity," Rohan emphasized, "is that **debt costs are tax-deductible, making the effective cost lower than nominal rates. Equity typically costs more but doesn't create repayment obligations that could strain cash flow during difficult periods**."

"The optimal approach is usually a balanced capital structure enough equity to provide stability and enough debt to enhance returns without creating excessive risk. This balance depends on your industry, growth rate, cash flow predictability, and risk tolerance."

"What's the ideal debt-to-equity ratio for a tech startup?" Jay inquired.

"There's no universal answer," Rohan replied. "Technology companies often favor equity-heavy structures initially due to uncertain early-stage revenues and the need for rapid scaling. As you establish predictable revenue streams, introducing debt can enhance returns to equity investors without compromising stability."

Vijay appreciated the clay cup not just for its flavor enhancement but for its environmental sustainability—a thoughtful touch that reflected the kind of business consciousness he hoped to embody.

"The Indian government has created special initiatives for startups and MSMEs, and rightly so, since the Indian MSME sector, comprising over 63 million enterprises, contributes 30% of Indian GDP," Rohan continued. Registering as a startup brings benefits like reduced fees for intellectual property filings, tax advantages, and simplified compliance. MSME registration provides access to government-guaranteed loan schemes with favorable terms, protection against delayed payments from larger companies, and preferential treatment in government procurement."

Vijay, drawing on his international perspective, asked, "Could my US entity provide a loan to our Indian venture at the 5% rate available in America? That seems significantly lower than Indian rates."

"Yes, that's possible through External Commercial Borrowing,"

Rohan confirmed. ECBs allow Indian businesses to access foreign debt, subject to RBI guidelines under FEMA. While 5% would be attractive compared to domestic rates, remember to factor in foreign exchange risk—the effective cost could increase if the rupee depreciates against the dollar during the loan term. This risk can be managed through hedging instruments, though they add to your overall cost."

Vijay found the coffee so enjoyable that he ordered another round for himself and offered refills to his cousins. As their fresh beverages were prepared, Rohan added a crucial piece of advice.

"Beyond domestic and cross-border debt, explore funds registered outside India that invest in Indian ventures through equity or convertible instruments like Compulsorily Convertible Preference Shares. These investments are permitted subject to RBI reporting and FEMA valuation guidelines."

As they received their second round of drinks, Rohan concluded with a measured warning. "Like coffee, which can be delightful in moderation but problematic in excess, funding must be approached with balance. Excessive debt can lead to insolvency if repayment becomes challenging, while excessive equity dilution reduces your returns and potentially your control. The art lies in finding the optimal mix for your specific situation."

Vijay savored his second kulhad of coffee, appreciating both the traditional container and Rohan's apt analogy. "You've given us a comprehensive overview of the funding landscape," he acknowledged. "Having these options mapped out gives us a tremendous strategic advantage as we plan our capital structure."

"I'm happy to help further when you reach the specific funding stage," Rohan offered. "Financial structuring is both art and science—and getting it right from the beginning creates a foundation for sustainable growth."

The three cousins finished their beverages, returned the empty kulhads, and headed back toward their hotel. The evening sky was beginning to darken, painting Prayagraj in soft twilight hues as millions of pilgrims continued their spiritual journeys against this magnificent backdrop. Similarly, Jay and Vijay felt their entrepreneurial journey taking a more definite shape, illuminated by Rohan's financial wisdom.

SUMMARY

It is very important to fund a business at the right time. Funding can be through debt, which comes with a fixed interest cost and repayment obligation. Equity is the safest form of funding for business. It can be brought by the entrepreneur or through dedicated Alternative Investment Funds (AIFs) willing to put capital into the business for growth and value creation, which all the contributors of the business will ultimately share.

There are reporting and approval routes to bring foreign capital into India.

CHAPTER

10

SUCCESS MANTRA OF BUSINESS

That evening, the brothers decided to witness the spectacular Ganga Aarti performed at one of the ghats in Mahakumbh. The ceremonial worship of the River Ganga was a breathtaking experience—hundreds of priests moving in synchronized motions, holding large flaming lamps that created dancing reflections on the sacred waters. Thousands of small diyas (oil lamps) floated on the river, creating a river of light that mirrored the star-studded sky above.

As their final night in Prayagraj, this spiritual culmination seemed the perfect backdrop for Rohan to share his most personal business wisdom—the success mantras he had distilled from years of entrepreneurial triumphs and failures.

After returning to their hotel and enjoying a light dinner, they gathered in Rohan's room. The windows were slightly ajar, allowing the distant sounds of devotional songs to filter through, creating an atmosphere that blended business pragmatism with spiritual reflection.

"Before we part ways tomorrow," Rohan began, settling into a comfortable chair. At the same time, his cousins took seats across from him. "I want to share four success formulas that have emerged from my business journey—principles that have made all the difference between my early failures and subsequent successes."

Jay and Vijay leaned forward attentively, notebooks ready, sensing that these insights represented the distillation of Rohan's most hard-won wisdom.

"The first principle is the smart deployment of money," Rohan stated, his voice taking on the gravity of a guru imparting essential teachings. "Having discussed various funding sources yesterday, understand that how you deploy capital is even more important than how you raise it."

He paused, organizing his thoughts before continuing. **"An entrepreneur needs a clear roadmap with specific milestones**—product development phases, service launch timelines, revenue targets, marketing campaigns, expansion points, potential acquisitions, capital expenditure needs, and working capital management. Each milestone should have defined capital requirements and expected returns."

Rohan's expression reflected the seriousness of this principle. "Money deployed strategically generates higher returns than money deployed reactively. I've seen competitors with greater funding fail because they allocated capital inefficiently, while more capital-constrained businesses thrived through disciplined deployment."

Jay nodded, making notes while Vijay listened intently, mentally connecting these principles to patterns he'd observed in Silicon Valley startups.

"The second principle is operational efficiency," Rohan continued. "In today's digital landscape, geography no longer constrains business operations. For instance, Vijay could operate the Indian company's bank account from Texas after completing the bank's KYC requirements. Since NRIs typically don't have Aadhar cards, the process would be passport-based, but entirely achievable remotely."

Rohan shared practical examples of operational efficiencies that are now available to Indian businesses. "Digital banking has eliminated the need for physical branch visits. The Unified Payment Interface (UPI) system allows customer payments to be received in seconds through simple QR codes. International recognition of India's UPI system has led countries like Singapore and the UAE to adopt similar systems for cross-border transactions. Unlike traditional banking with high fees, UPI transactions are either free or minimally priced, democratizing financial access."

He leaned forward, emphasizing his point. "Modern collaboration tools like Microsoft Teams, Google Meet, or Zoom enable seamless virtual meetings with colleagues, customers, and vendors worldwide. I have a friend who is the director of an Indian subsidiary of a German multinational. Their board meetings occur in Germany, and Indian directors participate virtually. This technology eliminates geographical barriers, saving time and increasing operational efficiency."

Jay could see the immediate applicability to their planned venture with team members across continents.

The third principle," Rohan stated firmly, "is that non-compliance is entirely avoidable and inexcusable in today's environment. Some misguided entrepreneurs view compliance as an unnecessary cost, but I consider it a smart investment that prevents catastrophic penalties and interest."

His tone conveyed the seriousness of this principle. "**All tax departments now offer online payment systems** for withholding taxes, income tax, GST, professional tax, provident fund, ESI, stamp duty, and virtually all government charges. Returns can be filed online and validated through OTP or digital signatures."

Rohan shared his approach. I maintain a reliable chartered accountant who ensures all compliance requirements for both my businesses are met. My office provides necessary data to the CA's team well before deadlines, ensuring timely payments and filings. I'm proud that we've never received government notices due to our perfect compliance record."

He emphasized the business advantage of compliance. "**Beyond avoiding penalties, timely compliance facilitates fundraising. Investors perform due diligence on business records, and compliance lapses can terminate investment discussions immediately**. Serious investors avoid businesses with careless attitudes toward regulatory requirements."

"Finally," Rohan said, his expression softening slightly, "the fourth principle is maintaining robust Management Information Systems. Every business owner needs accessible, accurate, and timely information about business performance."

"Whether standardized reports from accounting systems or custom dashboards designed by experts, good MIS delivers critical insights to your desktop or mobile device, enabling quick, informed decisions."

Rohan concluded with a saying that clearly held deep meaning for him: "Taking the right decision is 50% of success, but making a timely decision is 100% of success. Without proper MIS, neither is possible."

As Rohan finished sharing these principles, a comfortable silence fell over the room, punctuated only by distant temple bells. These weren't merely business tactics but a philosophy of entrepreneurship that balanced pragmatism with ethics, efficiency with compliance, and ambition with discipline.

Jay finally broke the silence. "Rohan bhai, these principles are invaluable. They're not taught in business schools but seem essential for real-world success."

Vijay nodded in agreement. "What strikes me is the integration of traditional business wisdom with modern technological advantages. Your approach blends timeless principles with contemporary tools."

Rohan smiled, pleased that his cousins had grasped the essence of his teaching. "Business fundamentals remain constant across generations and cultures. What changes are the tools, technologies, and regulatory environments? The successful entrepreneur honors the fundamentals while mastering the evolving landscape."

As the evening drew to a close, they knew tomorrow would bring their separation—Vijay returning to Texas via Delhi, Rohan to Mumbai, and Jay to Chennai. But something profound had been established during these three days at Mahakumbh

—not just spiritual renewal through the sacred waters, but the foundation of a business legacy that could span generations and potentially transform countless lives through their innovative technology.

SUMMARY

To succeed in the business, the following factors need to be considered.

- Smart deployment of money as per the growing needs of business.
- Operational efficiency should constantly be improved and integrated into the business.
- Compliance with the rule of the land is a must, else it can incur a heavy cost on the business
- A business owner should always look at the reporting numbers to understand the financial and operational efficiency of the business

CHAPTER

11

SYNOPSIS

Morning broke over Prayagraj with a serene beauty that belied the city's temporary transformation into the world's largest gathering. The cousins had packed their bags and prepared for departure. Though their flights were scheduled at different times—Vijay to Delhi at 2 PM, Rohan to Mumbai at 3 PM, and Jay to Chennai at 4 PM—they decided to leave for the airport together after breakfast at 9:30 AM to avoid potential traffic complications.

Their foresight proved wise. The roads were congested with departing pilgrims, creating substantial delays. Despite the slow progress, they maintained cheerful spirits, reflecting on their extraordinary experiences at Mahakumbh. They felt particularly fortunate to have participated in an event that occurs just once every 144 years—a cosmic alignment that seemed to mirror the alignment of their business aspirations.

They reached the airport by 11:30 AM, giving them ample time before their respective flights. They found a quiet corner in a restaurant at the terminal and ordered a light meal, using this final opportunity to consolidate the knowledge shared during their three days together.

"I can't thank you enough, Rohan bhai," Vijay said earnestly, "for taking the time to explain everything so comprehensively. What could have taken us months of research and likely many costly mistakes, you've condensed into a masterclass on Indian business."

Jay nodded in agreement. "You've made complex concepts accessible and practical. I feel genuinely prepared to embark on this journey once I complete my studies."

Rohan waved away their thanks with characteristic humility. "Teaching you both has been my privilege. The best way you can thank me is by building something remarkable—a business that creates value, employs people with dignity, and contributes to India's continued economic rise."

Vijay, ever the systematic thinker, wanted to ensure he had captured the essence of their discussions. "Let me summarize what I've understood from these three days to make sure I haven't missed anything crucial."

Rohan nodded encouragingly, pleased by his cousin's thoroughness.

"First," Vijay began, "establishing a business in India is now streamlined and accessible, even for operations with international connections. As the world's fifth-largest economy on a rapid growth trajectory, India offers tremendous opportunity."

"Second, we need to carefully determine the most appropriate entity structure for our specific circumstances—likely a private limited company given our international ownership and technology focus."

"Third, foreign investment in India is now welcome and straightforward, with most sectors requiring only reporting rather than prior approvals."

"Fourth, finding reliable consultants—legal, financial, and compliance—is essential to navigating regulatory requirements efficiently."

"Fifth, India's tax rates are actually quite competitive internationally, contrary to some misconceptions."

"And sixth, both entry and exit processes for businesses have been significantly simplified in recent years."

Jay added his key takeaways: "Beyond those structural points, I've learned the importance of maintaining financial discipline and operational efficiency throughout the business lifecycle. The success mantras you shared last night—smart capital deployment, operational streamlining, rigorous compliance, and effective management information systems—seem applicable to businesses of any size or sector."

Rohan nodded, pleased by their comprehension. "You've captured the essentials perfectly. Remember that these principles aren't just academic concepts but practical tools that will serve you daily as you build your venture."

As they finished their meal, Vijay and Jay insisted on paying the bill—a small gesture of appreciation for Rohan's priceless mentorship. The announcement for Delhi flights began to echo through the terminal, signaling the approaching moment of separation.

The three cousins stood, forming a tight circle away from the bustling terminal crowd. Their eyes glistened with emotion, not just from parting but from the profound sense that something significant had been established during their time together. The spiritual renewal of Mahakumbh had coincided with the birth of a business vision that now felt tangible and achievable.

Rohan reached into his briefcase one final time and handed each of his cousins printed copies of the three papers he had referenced throughout their discussions: "Essential Details about India," "Government Thrust and Policies," and "India – An Economic Powerhouse."

He advised, "Study these during your flights. They contain data and insights that will reinforce everything we've discussed."

As the final boarding call for Delhi flights echoed through the terminal, the three embraced warmly, their eyes moist but their hearts full. No elaborate goodbyes were necessary—they knew this wasn't an ending but the beginning of a shared journey that would unfold across continents, connecting three lives in purpose and vision.

Vijay departed first, turning back once to wave before disappearing into the security checkpoint. Rohan and Jay watched him go, their expressions reflecting both the sadness of separation and the excitement of what lay ahead.

At that moment, amid the chaos of the airport terminal, India's ancient wisdom seemed to converge with its modern potential—three rivers of individual talent flowing together to create something greater than their separate courses could achieve alone.

CHAPTER

12

ANNEXURES - THE KNOWLEDGE LEGACY

As Jay and Rohan watched Vijay disappear through the security checkpoint, Jay turned to his older cousin with newfound respect and admiration.

"You know, Rohan bhai, I've always looked up to you as a successful businessman, but these past days have shown me something more valuable—your capacity as a teacher and mentor."

Rohan smiled warmly. "Teaching forces clarity of thought. In explaining these concepts to you both, I've refined my understanding. That's the beauty of knowledge—unlike money, it multiplies when shared."

With time remaining before their flights, they found a quiet corner in the airport lounge. Jay opened one of the papers Rohan had given them, titled "Essential Details about India." As he began reading, his eyes widened at the comprehensive data Rohan had meticulously compiled.

"These papers are remarkable," Jay said, scanning the carefully organized information. "It's like you've distilled an entire course on India's economic landscape into these documents."

Rohan nodded. "Knowledge without context lacks power. These papers provide the factual foundation that supports everything we've discussed."

Jay's flight wouldn't leave for nearly two hours, so he began reviewing the documents in-depth, occasionally asking Rohan for clarification. The papers revealed a picture of India that went far beyond what most citizens understood about their own country.

Paper 1: Essential Details about India

The first paper detailed how India had transformed from a newly independent nation of 361 million people in 1951 to the world's most populous country with over 1.4 billion citizens. During this remarkable journey, per capita income had risen from just US$64 annually to US$2,601, while literacy rates had soared from 16.6% to 74%.

"I didn't realize we had reduced poverty so dramatically, even if economic inequality has increased," Jay noted, tracing a finger along a graph showing the declining poverty rates.

The document outlined India's governmental structure, with its three branches—executive, Legislature, and Judiciary—and the federal system distributing power between the union and states. It also highlighted India's remarkable linguistic diversity, with over 121 languages and 270 mother tongues, 22 of which were officially recognized.

What truly captured Jay's attention was the infrastructure section, detailing how public infrastructure had become the backbone of economic development. The paper showed exponential growth in infrastructure spending, with budget allocations rising to ₹10 lakh crore in 2023-24.

"I had no idea we had the second-largest road network globally," Jay marveled. "Or that 94% of our railway network is now electrified."

Rohan nodded. "Most Indians don't realize how far we've come. We have 84 operational airports now. Our renewable energy capacity makes us the fourth-largest globally. We're already the third-largest energy-consuming nation and have set ambitious targets: 500 gigawatts of renewable capacity, 5 million tons of green hydrogen annually, and a 45% emissions reduction by 2030."

The paper detailed India's maritime sector, comprising ports, shipping, shipbuilding, ship repair, and inland water transport systems. Twelve government-owned major ports and approximately 217 minor and intermediate ports handle about 95% of the country's trade by volume and 70% by value.

"The digital connectivity statistics are most relevant to your venture," Rohan pointed out. "Rural internet subscriptions increased by 200% between 2015 and 2021, compared to 158% in urban areas. And our Unified Payments Interface has revolutionized digital payments, becoming a global success story."

The paper concluded with notes on India's improving literacy rates—74.04% overall, 82.14% for males and 65.46% for females—and the unique hospitality culture embodied in the philosophy of "Atithi Devo Bhava" (The guest is God).

Paper 2: Government Thrust and Policies

As they waited for Rohan's flight announcement, Jay moved to the second paper, which outlined how India's stable government over the past 11 years had created unified policies that had yielded remarkable results in infrastructure development and living standards.

"The government's focus on ease of doing business is evident here," Jay observed, reading about the adoption of modern laws and decriminalization of various provisions. "Entry and exit processes requiring minimal government intervention, self-certification, digitally signed documents, faceless assessment—these create genuine confidence in the business community."

Rohan nodded. "The initiative list is particularly relevant to your venture."

Jay read through the government initiatives outlined in the document:

- Make in India: Boosting manufacturing and attracting foreign investment
- Digital India: Creating digital infrastructure, delivering services digitally, and increasing digital literacy
- Goods and Services Tax (GST): Creating a common national market and reducing the overall tax burden
- Startup India: Promoting new enterprises and fostering

innovation

- Production-Linked Incentive (PLI) Scheme: Developing core manufacturing sectors to global standards
- Industrial Zones/Software Technology Parks: Designated areas for industry or technology companies, available at concessional rates with complete ecosystem support

"The section on women entrepreneurship is encouraging, too," Jay noted. "The Women Entrepreneurship Portal hosts information and services, providing crucial content, workshops, and campaigns."

Rohan checked his watch. "My flight boards soon. Let's quickly review the third paper, which is perhaps the most compelling."

Paper 3: India – An Economic Powerhouse

The final document painted a picture of India's economic trajectory that left Jay feeling both proud and inspired.

"Currently ranked as the world's fifth-largest economy by nominal GDP and third-largest by purchasing power parity," Jay read aloud. "Expected to surpass Japan and Germany to become the world's third-largest economy by 2027."

The paper cited global analysts declaring India the next great economic power: Goldman Sachs predicting it would become the world's second-largest economy by 2075, and the Financial Times's Martin Wolf suggesting that by 2050, India's purchasing power would be 30% larger than that of the United States.

"The economic data is compelling," Jay said, scanning the document. "Consistent growth since independence, rising per capita income, reduced poverty and infant mortality, improved human development indicators, and a shift from agriculture toward manufacturing and services."

The paper highlighted the 1991 economic reforms that opened India to foreign investors, reduced tariffs and interest rates, and privatized some public sector industries, creating the foundation for today's economic dynamism.

"The consumer boom section is particularly relevant to your business planning," Rohan pointed out. "With 1.4 billion people and countless unmet needs, India's growth is driven mainly by domestic consumption and investments. Real wages are growing at 4.6%, disposable income is growing in excess of 15%, and industries mature in the West are fast-growing here."

Jay's eyes widened at the demographic dividend section. "By 2030, India's working-age population is expected to be 1.04 billion with a dependency ratio at just 31.2%—the lowest in our history—contributing nearly a quarter of the incremental global workforce. And this advantage lasts until 2055!"

"And note this," Rohan said, pointing to a particular paragraph. "India has the largest pool of English-speaking STEM graduates in the world—your potential talent pool for your technology venture."

The wealth generation statistics were equally impressive—85,698 High net worth of Individuals with at least US$1 million in investable assets, placing India fourth globally behind only the US, China, and Japan. The ultra-high-net-worth individuals (those with assets exceeding US$100 million) had surpassed 100,000 for the first time globally.

"And finally," Rohan said as his flight was announced, "note that the market capitalization of publicly traded companies in India has surpassed Hong Kong and now stands at number four globally."

As Rohan gathered his belongings to board his flight, Jay stood respectfully, overwhelmed with gratitude.

"These documents are treasures, Rohan bhai," he said earnestly. "Combined with everything you've taught us, they give us not just knowledge but vision—a map to build something truly significant."

Rohan embraced his younger cousin warmly. "Knowledge is the only treasure that grows when shared. Use it wisely, build ethically, and remember that business success is meaningful only when it creates value for others."

They walked together toward Rohan's gate, their conversation turning to family matters and plans to reunite soon. As they reached the security checkpoint, Rohan made one final observation.

"You know, Jay, what happened these past days at Mahakumbh was special beyond words. The sacred confluence of rivers mirrors what's happening with the three of us—different talents, experiences, and perspectives flowing together to create something more powerful than our efforts could achieve alone."

Jay nodded, deeply moved by the metaphor. "The Triveni Sangam of entrepreneurship."

"Exactly," Rohan smiled. "Now go build something remarkable."

With a final embrace, Rohan disappeared into the security checkpoint, leaving Jay alone with the precious knowledge documents and a heart full of inspiration. As he walked back toward his gate, he felt not the heaviness of responsibility but the lightness of purpose and possibility.

The Mahakumbh pilgrimage had cleansed more than his spirit—it had clarified his vision, strengthened his resolve, and connected him to a legacy of business wisdom that would guide his entrepreneurial journey. In his hands, he held not just papers but a blueprint for the future, crafted with care by a cousin who had transformed from a successful businessman in his eyes to a true guru of enterprise.

Jay found a quiet seat near his gate and opened his laptop. Even before his flight departed, he began drafting an outline for the business plan that would bring their vision to life. On his screen, he typed a simple working title that captured everything these transformative days had inspired:

"Titans of Tomorrow: Democratizing Supply Chain Intelligence for a Rising India"

The journey of a thousand miles begins with a single step. As the boarding announcement for his flight echoed through the terminal, Jay took that step with confidence, clarity, and conviction—qualities forged in the sacred waters of Triveni Sangam and in the wisdom shared by a brother who believed in his potential to create something truly remarkable.

I’m truly grateful that you spent your time with my words.

Every author grows through the voices of their readers. As my journey as an author takes shape, I warmly invite your feedback and reflections on this book.

Your suggestions will inspire future writings that serve the business community even better.

You can connect with me at_

pranav@winadvisors.co.in

+91 9820469825

www.ingramcontent.com/pod-product-compliance
Lightning Source LLC
LaVergne TN
LVHW091519200926
848483LV00002B/253
* 9 7 9 8 9 0 1 7 6 3 3 0 8 *